ESSENTIAL TIPS 101

DECORATING WITH FABRIC

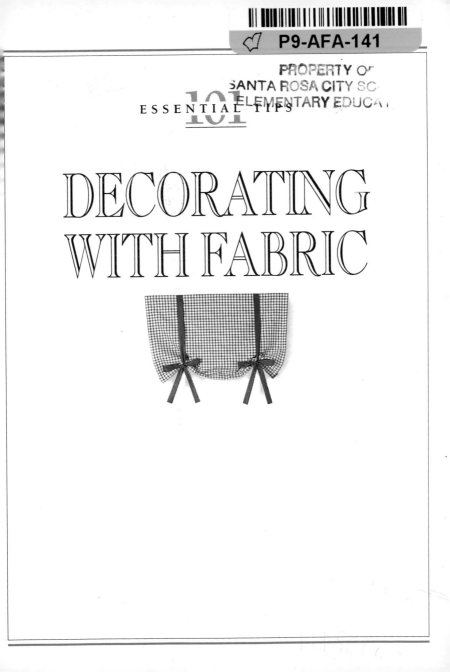

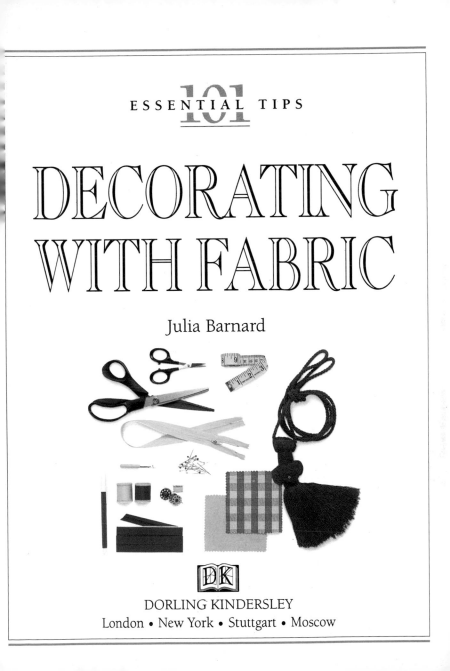

ESSENTIAL TIPS
101

DECORATING
WITH FABRIC

Julia Barnard

DK

DORLING KINDERSLEY
London • New York • Stuttgart • Moscow

A DORLING KINDERSLEY BOOK

Editor Susie Behar
Art Editor Colin Walton
Series Editor Charlotte Davies
Managing Art Editor Amanda Lunn
Production Controller Louise Daly
US Editor Laaren Brown

First American edition 1995
2 4 6 8 10 9 7 5 3 1
Published in the United States by
Dorling Kindersley Publishing, Inc.
95 Madison Avenue
New York, New York 10016

Distributed by Houghton Mifflin Company, Boston.

ISBN 0–7894–0171–1

Computer page makeup by Colin Walton Graphic Design, Great Britain
Text film output by Cooling Brown, Great Britain
Reproduced by Colourscan, Singapore
Printed and bound by Graphicom, Italy

ESSENTIAL 101 TIPS

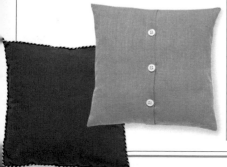

CURTAINS

1 CHOOSING A STYLE

A window is very often the focal point of a room, and the way it is dressed will set the style for the room. Your first decision will be whether to hang curtains or shades. When making your choice, take into account the size of the window, how much light or privacy you want, and how much money you are prepared to spend. For example, an elaborate dressing for a large window, which uses generous amounts of fabric, will be very expensive.

CORD TIEBACK

2 SIMPLE STYLES

One advantage of choosing a simple style of window dressing is the low cost. Roman or roller shades or unlined cotton fabric hung on a pole with rings or ties – these are all inexpensive. Some rooms, such as kitchens, and small rooms like studies, actually suit simple window treatments. If you want maximum light, but don't want to use tiebacks, hang curtains on a pole that is wider than the window frame.

△ PRACTICAL KITCHEN CURTAINS
The matching looped headings on the shade and curtains make them easy to take down and clean, a practical option for a kitchen.

◁ SIMPLE & DECORATIVE
The simple scalloped heading on this curtain adds decorative interest.

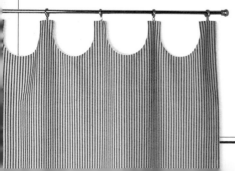

3 ELABORATE STYLES

A large window in a large room can usually take an opulent window dressing. Similarly, make a feature of a hallway by dressing the window sumptuously. Dress high windows with swags and tails, and plain windows with generous drapes, cornices or valances, and tiebacks.

△ GRAND & FORMAL
The strong lines of this window dressing, complete with the grand sweep of the swags and tails, fringe, rope, and tassels all create an air of old-world formality.

◁ COMBINE SHADES & CURTAINS
Even a small window can look impressive with the addition of an elaborate window treatment. The shade screens light and gives privacy; the drapes are for effect.

4 UNUSUAL USES FOR CURTAINS

In addition to being window treatments, curtains make excellent screens and are ideal for dividing a room into separate units; and in addition to being functional, they introduce a decorative element. When using curtains as screens, choose a simple hanging system.

- Create separate living space and sleeping areas in a studio by dividing the room with curtains.
- When you want just one living area, tie the curtains back.
- Cover up messy shelving with a pair of curtains. They will also form a screen against dust.

5 HIDDEN HANGING SYSTEMS

None of these hanging systems will show when the curtain is hung. Most are suitable for lightweight curtains. Optional track fittings, such as extension brackets, enable hanging systems to fit all openings.

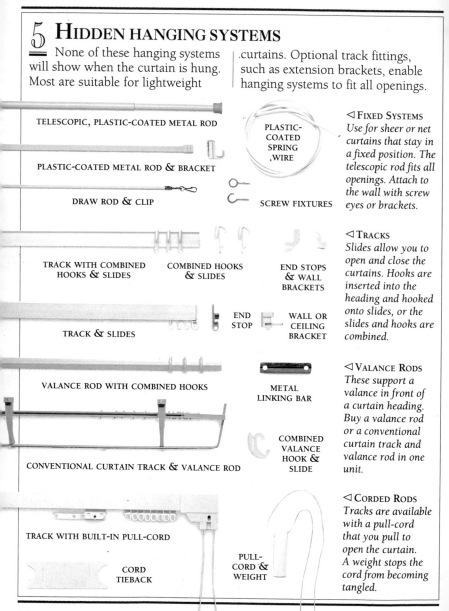

TELESCOPIC, PLASTIC-COATED METAL ROD

PLASTIC-COATED SPRING WIRE

PLASTIC-COATED METAL ROD & BRACKET

DRAW ROD & CLIP

SCREW FIXTURES

◁ **FIXED SYSTEMS**
Use for sheer or net curtains that stay in a fixed position. The telescopic rod fits all openings. Attach to the wall with screw eyes or brackets.

TRACK WITH COMBINED HOOKS & SLIDES

COMBINED HOOKS & SLIDES

END STOPS & WALL BRACKETS

◁ **TRACKS**
Slides allow you to open and close the curtains. Hooks are inserted into the heading and hooked onto slides, or the slides and hooks are combined.

TRACK & SLIDES

END STOP

WALL OR CEILING BRACKET

VALANCE ROD WITH COMBINED HOOKS

METAL LINKING BAR

◁ **VALANCE RODS**
These support a valance in front of a curtain heading. Buy a valance rod or a conventional curtain track and valance rod in one unit.

COMBINED VALANCE HOOK & SLIDE

CONVENTIONAL CURTAIN TRACK & VALANCE ROD

TRACK WITH BUILT-IN PULL-CORD

◁ **CORDED RODS**
Tracks are available with a pull-cord that you pull to open the curtain. A weight stops the cord from becoming tangled.

CORD TIEBACK

PULL-CORD & WEIGHT

6 DECORATIVE HANGING SYSTEMS

These systems form part of the visible window dressing. They range from simple wooden rods to ornate wrought iron rods. Hang your curtains with matching rings kept on the pole by decorative finials.

WOODEN ▷
These come with matching wooden fixtures that secure the pole firmly to the wall.

WOODEN SIDEWALL FIXTURES

SUPPORT ARM

WOODEN POLE WITH CURTAIN RINGS & FINIAL

BRASS ▷
These are available in a great range of diameters and so are suitable for nearly all types of curtain fabric.

BRASS SIDEWALL FIXTURES

BRASS SUPPORT ARMS

SMALL DIAMETER POLE

LARGE DIAMETER POLE

IRON ▷
Rods made from wrought iron are very decorative and can have ornately designed finials. Purchase them from shops or have them custom-made.

IRON ROD WITH CAGE FINIAL

IRON MOUNTING BRACKET

IRON ROD WITH CURVED FINIAL

7 CHOOSING A HANGING SYSTEM

It is important to decide on a hanging system before you buy the curtain fabric because the way you choose to hang the curtains will affect their length and width and thus the quantity of fabric that you require. Consider the style and size of both the window and room.

■ Make sure that the rod or track is long enough for your windows; it is not practical to join lengths of track.
■ If the room has curved or bay windows, choose a track that can be bent around the window frame.
■ Make sure that the track is strong enough for your curtains.

8 WHICH LENGTH?

Before measuring, consider the ideal length of curtain for the window. Curtains can hang to the windowsill, just past the sill, or to the floor. The size of the window and the style of the room influence the length. For example, an elaborate room needs full-length curtains, while simple, sill-length drapes will suit a small bedroom.

SILL LENGTH

APRON LENGTH

FLOOR LENGTH

△ LENGTH OPTIONS
The same size window can take sill-length, apron-length, or floor-length curtains, depending on the desired effect.

9 HOW TO MEASURE

For floor-length curtains, measure from the curtain rail or track to the floor (B). For windowsill-length, hang curtains ½ in (12 mm) above the sill or to apron length 2–4 in (5–10 cm) below (C). Add 3 in (7.5 cm) for the rod sleeve and 6 in (15 cm) for the lower hem. For the fabric width, multiply the span of the hanging system (A) by the fullness of the heading tape (*see p.14*). Add 12 in (30 cm) for side turnings. Divide this measurement by the fabric width for the number of panels needed.

CLOTH TAPE MEASURE

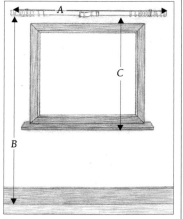

MEASURING THE LENGTH
Measure from the hanging system, not from the top of the window.

10 HOW TO MATCH FABRIC PATTERNS

Consider the placement of the fabric pattern in relation to the finished treatment. As you will nearly always need to join panels, measure the pattern repeat so that you can match the pattern across the seams.

HOW TO MEASURE THE PATTERN REPEAT
Lay the fabric on a flat surface and measure the distance between identical motifs.

11 MATCHING ACROSS CURTAINS

When you make a pair of curtains, make sure that the pattern matches across the drop from curtain to curtain. Calculate the pattern repeat and cut out the first curtain. Match the second to the first.

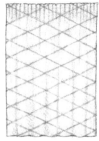

MATCH PATTERNS EDGE-TO-EDGE

12 METHODS FOR CUTTING FABRIC

Cut most fabrics with a pair of sharp scissors along a straightedge. Fine, loose-weave fabrics, such as muslin, can be cut using the pull-thread method (*see below*).

△ **CUTTING PATTERNED FABRIC**
Cut along the grain. Lay a try square at right angles to the finished edge and mark a cutting line with a vanishing-ink pen.

◁ **LOOSE-WEAVE FABRICS**
Make a cut through the finished edge. Gently pull out a single thread. The pulled thread will leave a guideline along which to cut.

13 WHICH HEADING?

Once you have chosen the fabric for your curtains, you must decide on the heading. This will affect the fullness, hang, and overall style of the window treatment. Ready-made heading tapes are available in a variety of gathered or pleated styles and in narrow or deep widths. Deep tapes allow you to hide the curtain rail or track. Most headings can be used either with hooks and tracks or hung on rings from decorative poles. Some headings require special hooks. Check this when you buy the heading tape.

SHEER & NET TAPE
A tape made specifically for sheer or net curtains. Allow for twice the track length.

GATHERED HEADING
Best suited to small curtains. Allow for one and a half to two times the track length.

PENCIL PLEATING
This tape produces multiple folds. Allow two and a half times the track length.

TRIPLE PINCH PLEATING
Use this tape with full-length curtains. Allow for twice the track length.

SMOCKED PLEATING
Suitable for valances and curtains, allow for two and a half times the track length.

CARTRIDGE PLEATING
Creates cylindrical pleats; best for long curtains. Allow for twice the track length.

BOX PLEATING
Suitable for fixed curtains and valances. Allow for three times the track length.

14 HOW TO MAKE A LOOPED HEADING

Some curtain styles do not require heading tape. Cut the fabric to the size required and join the pieces with flat fell seams (see p.63). Hem the sides and bottom. Cut as many loops as you need at double the length and width required. Add ⅝ in (1.5 cm) for seams. You will need a facing strip 2½ in (6 cm) wide plus 1¼ in (3 cm) for turnings.

1 Fold the loop strips lengthwise, right sides facing. Sew ⅝ in (1.5 cm) from the edge. Press seams open. Turn right sides out.

2 If narrow, stitch a thread to one end, pass it through the tube and pull. Press with the seam in the middle of one side.

3 Fold in half, seams to the inside. Tack to the right side of the curtain. Pin facing wrong side up with the raw edges aligned.

4 The loops are now sandwiched between facing and curtain. Sew a seam ⅝ in (1.5 cm) from the top. Fold under ⅝ in (1.5 cm) on the other edges of the facing. Tack.

5 Press the facing strip and curtain, wrong sides together. Slipstitch (see p.61) the folded edges of the facing to the curtain.

SIMPLE LOOPED HEADING ▷

15 HOW TO JOIN CURTAIN PANELS

Take accurate measurements. Before you start to cut, consider the pattern alignment across the finished panels. Cut one piece, and the second to match the first. Fold the hem and sides of the fabric by ⅝ in (1.5 cm) to the wrong side and press in place. Fold the sides over again by 1 in (2.5 cm) and press. Fold up the hem by 3 in (7.5 cm). Miter the corners (see p.65). Slipstitch the sides.

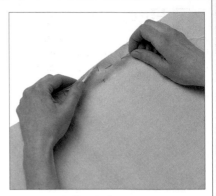

ATTACH MATCHING PANELS

16 HOW TO SECURE THE HEADING TAPE

When you choose a heading tape, remember that it will affect the way the curtains hang. Measure and cut the heading tape to the width of the curtains, adding ¾ in (2 cm) at each end to turn under. When you machine-sew the tape in place, sew the top and bottom edge in the same direction to prevent the fabric from puckering. Turn over the top edge of the fabric to the same length as the heading tape, less ⅜ in (1 cm).

1 Pin and press the top edge of the curtain fabric over to the wrong side. Lay the tape on the fold with its top edge just below the top fold.

2 Turn the sides under. Keep the drawstrings free at the side edge and knot them at the leading edge. Tack the top and bottom edges in place.

3 Pin and tack the ends of the tape in place. Machine sew along the top and bottom and side edges of the tape to secure to the curtain.

17 HOW TO HEM A CURTAIN

A curtain needs to be hemmed properly if it is to hang well. Heavy, lined curtains, in particular, look better if they are weighed down. Weights are available either as single button-shaped disks that are secured in the mitered corners or as chains that are sewn into the hem.

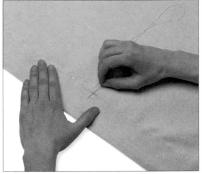

CHAIN WEIGHT

BUTTON WEIGHT

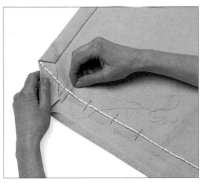

△ USING WEIGHTS
Unfold the hem so that the topmost fold is exposed. Lay the length of chain weights along the crease in the fabric. Oversew the weights in place at regular intervals.

△ FINISHING OFF THE HEM
Refold the hem and pin it in place. Slipstitch along the hem. Or neaten a once-turned hem with zigzag stitch and secure with herringbone stitch (see p.63).

18 GATHERING THE TAPE

Before you fit the curtain hooks and hang the curtain, you need to gather the heading tape. Grasp the ends of the drawstrings at the side of the curtain and pull the strings to one side. The tape will gather and form pleats. Ease the pleats along the length of the tape until the heading is gathered to the required width. Tie the ends of the drawstrings in a slipknot. You are now ready to thread the hooks.

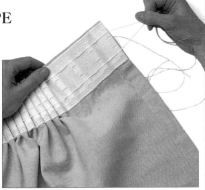

PULL DRAWSTRINGS TO ONE SIDE

19 WHEN TO LINE A CURTAIN

Add lining to your curtains to provide insulation, greater body, an extra screen against light, and to help keep them clean. Curtains that are made out of heavyweight fabric hang especially well when lined. If you want your curtains to provide good insulation, try interlining. This is when an appropriate material is inserted between the lining and curtain fabric. Make sure that you choose a lining that can be washed in the same way as the curtain, unless it is detachable.

20 HOW TO LINE A CURTAIN

Cut out panels for the curtain and join with plain flat seams (see p.62). Cut out panels for the lining, making them 5 in (13 cm) shorter than the curtain. Allow 3½ in (9 cm) at the hem edge and 1½ in (4 cm) at the heading. Join the panels of lining fabric with plain flat seams and trim 1½ in (4 cm) from each side of the lining panels. Turn under the sides and hem of lining by ⅝ in (1.5 cm). Turn curtain fabric sides under by 1½ in (4 cm). Turn a 2 in (5 cm) hem along the bottom edge. Miter the corners (see p.65).

1 Sew the hem of the curtain fabric using herringbone stitch.

2 Draw full-length vertical lines with tailor's chalk at intervals of about 12 in (30 cm) along the wrong side of the curtain.

3 Tack the lining to the curtain (wrong sides facing) along the lines, 6 in (15 cm) from the top. Lockstitch (loose stitches wide apart) along the lines.

4 Remove the tacking. Pin, tack, and slipstitch (see p.61) the lining to the curtain at the sides and hem. Remove the tacking. Attach chosen heading.

21 ATTACHING A HEADING

Measure from the bottom edge up and mark the desired length of the curtain at the top of the fabric. Turn the fabric down at the mark and press. Cut the heading tape to the curtain width, adding 1½ in (4 cm) for a seam allowance.

1 △ Trim the lining at the top so that its edge aligns with the mark indicating the top of the curtain drop. Fold over the top of the curtain, covering the edge of the lining. Pin over the lining and press.

2 Lay the heading below the top fold of the curtain. Knot the drawstring ends, turn under the end of the tape, and align the fold with the curtain edge. Sew as for an unlined curtain (see p.17).

22 MAKING A LOOSE-LINED CURTAIN

Cut the lining fabric to the size of the finished, ungathered curtain. Turn under the sides by ⅝ in (1.5 cm) twice and machine sew. Fold the lining heading tape double along its length. Pin the lining into the fold of the tape. Sew along the top and bottom edges in the same direction to prevent puckering. Gather the lining (see p.17) and hook it to the heading tape. Hem the lining by machine, making it 1½ in (4 cm) shorter than the curtain, allowing for a double hem of ⅝ in (1.5 cm).

DETACHABLE LINING
This is an ideal lining for curtains that need frequent cleaning. Unhook from the heading tape, remove the hooks, and ungather.

23 WHY HANG SHEER CURTAINS?

Some people do not like sheer curtains, even if it means that they forfeit privacy. If you want privacy but do not like the look of net, combine a translucent shade (which lets in light) with tied-back curtains, which are drawn at night.

- Use net curtains creatively by gathering them fully to diffuse light.
- Instead of net, hang a sheer fabric, such as muslin or eyelet.
- Colored sheer fabric curtains allow some light into a room as well as adding tone and color.

24 MAKING A SHEER CURTAIN

Use wide pieces of fabric so there are few joins. Cut straight by pulling along a single thread (see p.13). If you have to join widths, use French seams, allowing ⅝ in (1.5 cm). To make a French seam, machine sew a plain seam ³⁄₁₆ in (5 mm) from the edge. Trim the allowances to ⅛ in (3 mm). Turn the pieces right sides together and fold along the seam. Press. Sew a second seam ⅜ in (1 cm) from the first, enclosing the raw edges. Unfold, right side up. Press the seam to one side.

1 Lay the fabric on a flat surface. Neaten edges by pinning a ⅜ in (1 cm) double hem at each side edge. Sew and press hems.

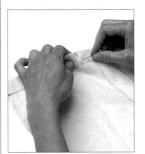

2 Pin a ¾-in (2-cm) double hem at the bottom edge. Sew and press the hem. At the top edge, turn over the fabric to the same width as the heading and pin in place.

3 Turn under ends of the tape by ¾ in (2 cm). Sew to curtain. Sew across the thread ends at the leading edge. Gather tape.

THE FINISHED CURTAIN ▷

25 WIRE FOR NET CURTAINS

A plastic-coated wire is suitable for hanging fixed-position net curtains. The wire is attached by a hook and eye to the sides of the frame.

SCREW EYES   PLASTIC-COATED SPRING WIRE

1 Mark the position for the eyes and push the awl into the marks to make pilot holes.

2 Screw the eyes into the wood. Measure the distance between the eyes and cut the wire to fit.

3 Screw the hooks into the ends of the wire. Clip the hooks to the eyes on the sides of the frame.

26 ATTACH A FRAME-MOUNTED TRACK

You can attach a curtain track to the wall above the frame or, if it is made of wood, to the frame itself. If the width of the frame makes it difficult to draw the curtains back, build a frame extension.

FRAME-MOUNTED TRACKS
Mark each bracket position. Make a pilot hole in each mark with an awl. Push the screw into the bracket and screw into place.

FRAME EXTENSIONS
To extend a window frame, attach a pair of wooden battens to the wall and then mount the brackets in place as before.

21

27 HOW TO MOUNT A TRACK

Cut the track to the size of the window frame, or longer if you want the curtains to overhang on each side. The track will be held in place by small brackets that are attached into the wall with a power drill, masonry bit, wallplugs, screws, and screwdriver. Before attaching the track, check that there is enough space between the frame and ceiling.

1 Draw a series of pencil marks along the top edge of the window, at an equal distance from the ceiling. Leave enough room to mount the track.

2 Join the pencil marks on the wall with a ruler. It is advisable to check the manufacturer's instructions for the right distance between brackets.

3 Allowing space for the overhang, mark the drilling positions with a pencil. Position the first bracket 2 in (5 cm) in from the end of the track.

4 Drill the first mark and push in a plug. Position the bracket and a screw and drive the screw tip into the wall anchor. Work along the points.

5 Check the alignment of the brackets and, depending on the type of track you have chosen, clip or slide it into place. Center over the window.

6 Once the track is correctly positioned on the wall, make it secure by tightening the screws on each bracket using a screwdriver.

28 SLIDES, HOOKS & END STOPS

Calculate the number of slides you need for the track. Slide them onto the track and then put on end stops or finials. You can buy slides and hooks combined that fit directly into the curtain. When you want to put the curtain up, remove the end stop. If you have too many slides, simply slip some of them off.

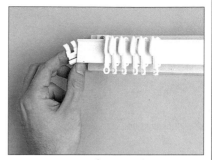

SLIDES & END STOP

29 HANGING & DRESSING

The way you hang curtains will affect the overall style of the room. Always hang heavy curtains for 48 hours before hemming them.

1 Thread hooks through pockets in the heading. Then hook them through eyelets in the bottom of each slide.

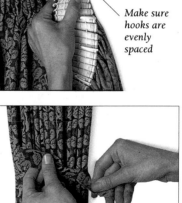

Make sure hooks are evenly spaced

2 Fold the curtain into accordion folds. Grasp each fold at the heading and pull down in one smooth action.

3 Tie the folds with fabric strips at the top, middle, and bottom. Do not tie too tightly. Remove after 48 hours.

30 HOLDBACKS

Holdbacks emphasize the folds of a curtain and, by pulling it back from the window, let in more light. They are available in a variety of designs in both wood and metal. Some are designed to match curtain poles. Buy them with screws and wall anchors.

Hook the fabric behind the holdback and decide on the best position.

— A decorative brass holdback

— The folds of the curtain fabric are emphasized by the holdback

— Carefully arranged folds create a formal effect

31 CORDS & TASSELS

Cords and tassels are available in all sizes and colors including multicolored. Attach a hook to the wall behind the curtain. Make it high enough to allow generous folds of curtain to hang below. Loop the tassel onto the hook and tie at the front. You can buy several different colored ropes and combine them to make a striking multicolored tassel.

Tie cord at front ⁄

Tassels come in all sizes, colors, and styles ——

Elegant folds of fabric below tassel ⁄

32 HOW TO MEASURE FOR A TIEBACK

First hang and dress the curtain. If it is made of a heavyweight fabric, let it hang for 48 hours. Pull back the curtain and hold a tape measure around it at the chosen level. Hold the ends of the tape against the wall where the hook is to be mounted. Note the measurement around the curtain and mark the hook position on the wall. It should be far enough from the window to let in as much daylight as possible.

MEASURING

33 HOW TO MAKE A V-SHAPED TIEBACK

To make this V-shaped tieback, you need fabric for the tieback and lining, interfacing, and suitable rings and hooks for attaching the tieback to the wall.

Begin by making a paper template. Measure for the tieback (*see p.24*). On the paper, mark a rectangle that is half the length of the tieback multiplied by 11 in (28 cm).

1 Cut out a wedge shape from the rectangle. Fold the fabric double. Place the pattern onto the fabric with the wide end of the wedge on the fold.

2 Cut out the fabric and lining, allowing for a seam. Cut the interfacing to fit the pattern. Unfold fabric. Lay right side down. Tack on the interfacing.

3 Place fabric and lining right side together. Sew together near the edge of the interfacing. Leave a gap to turn the fabric right side out.

4 Pull the tieback right side out. Turn in the raw edges of the gap and slipstitch them together. Topstitch the interfacing in place just inside the edge.

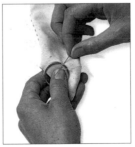

5 Oversew rings at the ends of the tieback. (The rings show if placed right at the edge.) Attach the hook to the wall and hang the tieback in place.

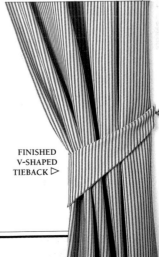

FINISHED
V-SHAPED
TIEBACK ▷

34 INTEGRAL VALANCE

Here, the heading tape is added once the valance is attached. Cut the fabric to the curtain width plus 4½ in (11 cm) for seams. Allow about one-sixth of the curtain drop for the length. Add ⅝ in (1.5 cm) for seams. Cut the lining 3 in (8 cm) less in width and to the same depth. Cut a fringe 2¼ in (5.5 cm) less than the length of the valance hem edge. Attach the fringe to the right side, facing away from the edge. Align the top edges of lining and fabric seams. Press seams and turn right side out.

1 Turn under the bottom edge of the lining by ⅝ in (1.5 cm). Press it and slipstitch along the back of the fringed edge.

2 Lay the curtain right side up with the valance on it. Pin and tack the valance to the curtain along the heading edge.

3 Cut a bias strip (see p.60) to the length of the valance. Align the strip with the top edge of the valance. Sew in place.

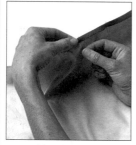

4 Fold and pin the bias over the raw edges of the valance and curtain. Slipstitch along the seam on the lined side.

5 Hand stitch the heading tape to the curtain just below the bound edge. Sew through all the fabric layers.

GATHERED VALANCE

35 VALANCE WITH BOUND EDGE

Cut out the fabric, allowing for side and heading turnings. Cut out the lining ¾ in (2 cm) smaller. Place right sides together and stitch side seams. Press the seams open and turn the fabric right side out. Fold the top 1½ in (4 cm) of fabric over the lining and press.

1 Lay the heading tape on the valance to align with the top edge. Sew the tape in place.

2 Attach a bias strip to the bottom of the valance (*see p.60*). Gather the heading tape.

THE FINISHED VALANCE

36 PUTTING UP A CORNICE BOARD

Unlike a flexible fabric valance, a cornice is made of rigid or semirigid material. It is hung over the window on a board supported by right-angled brackets. To attach the board to the wall, align it with the window or ceiling. Check the alignment with a level.

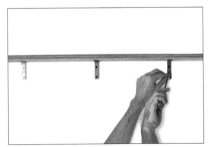

1 Mark drilling points through the holes. Remove the cornice board, drill the holes, and fix wall anchors.

2 Place the cornice board on the wall and align the brackets with the wall anchors. Screw the brackets into place.

37 HOW TO MAKE A SIMPLE CORNICE

A cornice is made from semi-rigid or rigid panels covered with fabric, which usually matches the curtains. It should be slightly wider, and its front far enough away from the curtains to ensure they do not drag against it when they are opened or closed. The depth of the cornice depends on the length and style of the curtain, but a good rule to follow is to make the cornice one-eighth the depth of the curtain. This cornice is made with buckram, a stiff burlap, which gives it a firm shape.

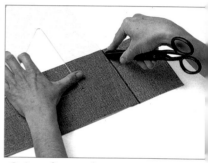

1 Measure the length and depth (wider and broader than the curtains) needed. Remember to include the sides. Cut the buckram to size with heavy-duty shears.

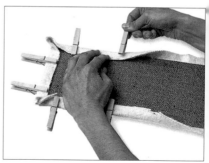

2 Score lines at the cornice corners. Cut out the interlining and lining ⅝ in (1.5 cm) and curtain fabric 1¼ in (3 cm) larger all around than the buckram.

3 Lay the buckram on the interlining and lightly dampen its edges with water using a paintbrush. The dampened buckram will become lightly adhesive.

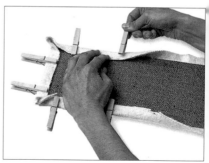

4 Fold over the edges of the interlining onto the edge of the buckram. Press the interlining edges down firmly, and hold in place with clothespins.

5 Press the edges over a damp cloth so that the interlining will adhere. Trim off the excess interlining at the corners.

6 Fold the fabric edges over the panel. Miter the corners. Smooth and pin in place. Iron the edges over a damp cloth.

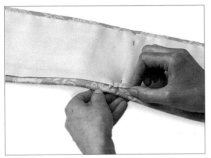

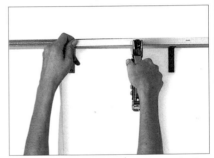

7 Turn the lining edges ¾ in (2 cm) to the wrong side. Miter corners and press. Slipstitch lining to panel back.

8 Cut Velcro tape to fit frame. Staple the hooked strip to the frame. Slipstitch the fuzzy strip to the top edge of the cornice.

9 Fold the fabric-covered panel along the scored lines. Attach to the board by pressing the Velcro strips together.

THE FINISHED CORNICE

SHADES

38 WHY USE SHADES?

Hanging shades is an ancient method of screening light from a room. Today they come in all shapes and sizes, ranging from simple roller shades to elaborate Austrian shades. Hang shades at windows that need to be screened but where insulation is not important or when you want maximum daylight to enter a room. Shades are also practical in rooms that require permanent screening.

RUCHED AUSTRIAN SHADE

39 HOW TO MEASURE FOR A SHADE

Choose the style of shade you want and then measure the window area. Shades can either be fixed within the recess, or they can cover the whole window area. If the shade is to fit within the recess, measure from the fixing position to the windowsill for the drop required. The width should be 1¼ in (3 cm) less than the width of the recess. For a shade that covers the whole window area, measure from the top of the hanging system to 2 in (5 cm) below the windowsill for the drop. The width should be 2 in (5 cm) wider than the window at each side.

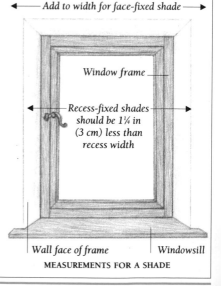

Add to width for face-fixed shade

Window frame

Recess-fixed shades should be 1¼ in (3 cm) less than recess width

Wall face of frame   Windowsill

MEASUREMENTS FOR A SHADE

40 TIE SHADE

Measure and add 2½ in (6 cm) all around for turnings. Mount the heading board in position (*see p.27*). If the shade is to be mounted in the recess, attach the board to the top of the recess with screws. Staple a strip of Velcro to the board. Make four fabric ties (*see p.67*), each 2 in (5 cm) longer than the shade. When the shade is complete, loosely gather the fabric and knot the ties.

1 Cut out the fabric and sew a ⅝-in (1.5-cm) double hem to the wrong side on the sides and bottom edge.

2 Lay out the fabric on a flat surface. Mark a quarter of the shade width from both corners on the top edge.

3 Sew the ties to the top edge of the fabric on both sides. Align them with the quarter marks.

4 Cut a Velcro strip to the shade width. Turn 1¼ in (3 cm) under along the top. Press and sew the strip to the edge.

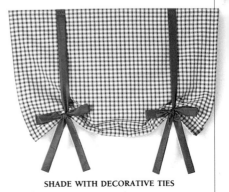

SHADE WITH DECORATIVE TIES

41 MAKING A SIMPLE ROLLER SHADE

A roller shade has a spring mechanism that enables it to roll up tightly, allowing maximum daylight into a room. Roller shade fabric needs to be stiff, so use a specially made roller shade fabric or buy a stiffener which, when applied to a thin fabric, will make it suitable. You can buy an entire roller shade kit for easy assembly. Measure up for the shade and add 12 in (30 cm) to the length to allow for the roller to be covered with fabric when the shade is down, and for the batten channel along the bottom edge. Cut the roller to the distance between the fixed brackets, less ⅛ in (3 mm) to allow for an end cap to be fitted. If you are hanging the shade within a recess, allow ¾ in (2 cm) from the top of the brackets to the recess. Align the brackets with the window.

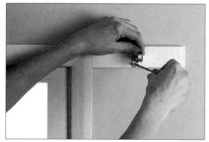

1 Fix the bracket for the square pin to the left, and the bracket for the round pin to the right.

2 Measure and cut out the fabric. Join widths by overlapping edges by ⅜ in (1 cm) and sew close to the raw edges.

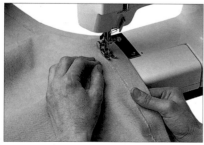

3 Finish the lower edge with zigzag stitch. Fold and machine-sew a channel for the batten. Leave the sides open.

4 Lay the fabric right side up with the roller in place. Tape the top along its length with double-sided tape.

5 Work a half-roll of fabric onto the roller and attach it with staples, following the manufacturer's instructions.

6 Insert the batten in the channel. Attach the cord holder on the wrong side of the fabric. Thread the weight onto the cord.

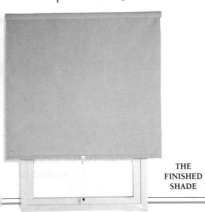

THE FINISHED SHADE

42 ADDING FRINGE EDGING

Brighten a simple roller shade with a decorative edging. Consider the size of the edging in relation to the window. If the roller is to be face-mounted, allow for the edging to drop well below the sill. If the shade is mounted within a recess, the edging should drop to the sill. Choose from the large selection of ready-made decorative edgings available.

1 Cut the fringe to the shade width. Add 2 in (5 cm) for turnings. Trim ends and turn them to the wrong side.

2 Remove batten. Slipstitch the fringe to the lower edge of the channel, the wrong side facing the shade's right side.

CUSHIONS

43 CHOOSING THE STYLE

Cushions bring color, texture, and style to a room and can dramatically affect its character. Add cushions to unify the color or theme of a room or to provide a splash of complementary or contrasting color. There are two main types of cushions: fitted cushions, such as box cushions, and scatter cushions. You can use almost any fabric to make cushions, ranging from antique tapestry to delicate silk.

SQUARE SCATTER CUSHION

44 CUSHION FILLINGS

If you want to make your own cushion pad, the first step is to choose a filling. A wide selection of natural fibers, such as feathers and down, or synthetic fillings, such as polyester, is available. Filling is usually sold as loose material by weight. The most comfortable and durable are natural fiber fillings, such as kapok. Synthetic fibers are not as soft and may lose their shape. Feathers feel luxurious, but can be messy to work with.

FOAM
Ideal for a seat cushion and easy to work with.

KAPOK
A vegetable fiber; durable, but may feel lumpy over time.

FIBERFILL
Synthetic; useful for filling pads of unusual shape.

POLYSTYRENE BEADS
Lightweight but firm; good for large floor cushions.

FEATHERS & DOWN
Soft and light; less expensive than pure down.

45 CUSHION PAD

The pad should be ⅝ in
(1.5 cm) larger than the cushion for
a plump effect. Choose a casing
fabric such as cambric, or even a
lining fabric. Make a paper pattern,
allowing ⅝ in (1.5 cm) for seams.

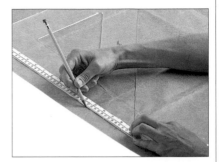

1 ▷ Pin the pattern to the casing fabric.
Cut out two identical pieces.

2 Sew three sides (right sides) together,
⅝ in (1.5 cm) from the edge. Sew
seams 2 in (5 cm) in from each corner.

3 Clip the corners of the seam to ¼ in
(6 mm) from the seam. Turn the
cushion pad right side out.

4 Stuff the filling into the pad. Push it
well into each corner and distribute it
evenly throughout the whole pad.

5 When the casing has been filled to
the required plumpness, slipstitch the
opening closed (see p.61).

46 MAKING A SQUARE CUSHION COVER

Square cushions make versatile accents in the home. You can buy or make them in an array of fabrics and with a range of stuffings and fastenings. The easiest fastening is slipstitching (*see below*), although this is not suitable if you need to wash the cover frequently. A wide variety of edgings, such as fringes or piping, are available.

1 Make a pattern the same size as the pad. Lay the pattern on a double layer of fabric. Pin the pattern in place and cut out the fabric pieces.

2 Align and pin the two panels along all four sides of the square (right sides together). Tack ⅜ in (1.5 cm) from the edge along three of the sides.

3 Stitch 2 in (5 cm) from both ends on side four. Machine-sew along edges near the tacking stitches. Do not stitch up opening. Remove tacking stitches.

4 Clip each corner diagonally to reduce fabric bulk. Cut away the seam to within ¼ in (6 mm) of the stitching to limit bulk and wrinkling.

5 Turn the cover right side out. Insert the inner pad through the cover opening and push it in. Slipstitch the opening (*see p.61*).

SQUARE CUSHION COVER

47 MAKING A SIMPLE ROUND CUSHION

To make a circular pattern for the cushion, use a plate (if it is the right size) or make a compass from a length of string, a pencil, and a push pin. Fold a piece of paper into quarters. Knot one end of the string and cut it to half the cushion diameter. Hold the knotted end at the inner corner and tie a pencil to the other end.

1 Draw an arc across the piece of paper with the homemade compass. Cut along the pencil mark. Unfold the pattern. Pin the paper to the fabric.

2 Cut out the front and back panels. Tack right sides together, leaving ⅝ in (1.5 cm) for seams and a gap large enough for the pad to be inserted.

3 Machine-sew the seam along the tacking. Be careful not to sew across the opening left for the pad. Take out the tacking stitches.

4 Cut notches around the seam allowance (see p.62). Turn the cover right side out and press. Insert the pad through the gap. Push it in well.

5 Close the opening with slipstitches. If you need to wash the cushion, it is easy to take out these stitches with a seam ripper or small scissors.

ROUND CUSHION COVER

48 HOW TO ADD A CORD EDGING

Liven up an old cushion by adding a cord edging. To establish the correct length, measure around the cushion and add 2 in (5 cm).

1 Make a seam opening ¾ in (2 cm) long. Tuck one end of the cord into the gap. Oversew. Slipstitch to the cushion edge.

2 Make simple loops at each of the corners by wrapping the cord around a pencil to ensure equal size. Oversew in place.

3 Finish sewing the cord around the edge. Tuck the end of the cord in the seam. Slipstitch the opening closed.

49 HOW TO ADD A FLANGE EDGING

The flange is made from the same fabric as the cushion. Make the opening in the back panel. Fasten with buttons, a zipper, or Velcro.

1 Add 2½ in (6 cm) to the panels for the flange and ⅝ in (1.5 cm) for the seam allowance. Join the panels (see p.39).

2 Turn the cover right side out. Mark a line 2 in (6 cm) from the edge in tailor's chalk. Tack and machine-sew.

3 If your machine does not have a double needle, stitch around the cushion along each side of the tacking stitches.

50 CUSHION WITH A ZIPPER

You will need to use a zipper that is 4 in (10 cm) shorter than the side of the cushion. Cut the two cushion cover panels to the desired size.

1 Sew a flat seam for the opening. Press the seam open along stitched and unstitched sections. Tack the zipper in place.

2 From the right side, slipstitch the opening together along the folded edges. Topstitch using the zipper foot attachment.

3 Stitch across the ends as close as possible to the tape ends to join the lines of topstitches. Remove the slipstitches.

51 BUTTON FASTENING

Unlike zippers or snaps, buttons can be an attractive feature of the back panel. (See page 66 for the method for making buttonholes.)

1 Cut out the cushion using a pattern (see p.36). Cut the pattern in half. Pin it to a double layer of fabric.

2 Cut two panels, adding 2 in (5 cm) for a center opening. Turn the center edges of backs under by ⅜ in (1 cm). Sew the edge.

3 Lay the panels right sides together. Overlap backs by 1 in (2.5 cm), the holed one underneath. Sew the panels together.

52 USING LIGHTWEIGHT FABRICS

Sewing very fine, lightweight fabrics requires special care:

▪ Lightweight fabrics should be backed for extra strength. Make sure that the backing is compatible with the fabric in weight and color.

▪ Always attach lace or other delicate edgings to a cushion by hand.

▪ Avoid using zippers on lace cushion covers.

▪ On shallow turnings in lightweight fabrics, the cover corners do not need mitering.

▪ Silk is light but durable and is ideal for making cushions. Line if it has a very fine weave.

SEWING DELICATE FABRICS
This fine lace and silk cushion has been hand sewn to prevent any damage from occurring to the fabric.

53 USING HEAVYWEIGHT FABRICS

Heavyweight fabrics, such as tapestry and Jacquard, make excellent cushion covers. Seek out old pieces of fabric from junk shops, or use rug fragments from worn-out oriental carpets or kilims. If the fabric has an open weave, it will need to be lined for added strength. A lining will also prevent the inner cushion pad from showing through gaps in the weave of the fabric. Heavyweight fabrics are ideal for making fitted cushions, such as bolsters and box cushions.

TAPESTRY CUSHIONS ▷
Tapestry creates a warm effect. Since the panels are rarely square, use the panel as a pattern for the whole cushion.

54 SEAT CUSHION WITH TIES

This seat cushion is filled with a foam padding 1½ in (4 cm) thick. Make a pattern of the seat chair with a sheet of tracing paper. Cut the tracing paper slightly larger than the seat area. Lay the paper on the seat and crease it over the edge. Pencil around the seat perimeter. Add piping trim to the finished cushion if desired (see p.60).

1 Once you have marked the perimeter, remove the paper and fold it in half to make sure it is equal on both sides.

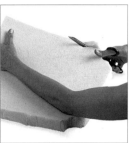

2 Unfold and lay the pattern on the foam. Cut out. Pin the pattern to the fabric. Cut out two panels, plus ⅝ in (1.5 cm).

Trim seams

3 Attach piping to the right side of the front panel. Sew together the right sides of both panels. Leave a gap for the pad.

4 Lay the cushion on the chair and mark where the ties should be placed. Make the ties (see p.66). Oversew each tie in position to the seam on the lower cushion panel.

5 Press the cushion cover and insert the foam pad through the opening. Turn in the seam allowances, align the edges, and slipstitch the opening closed.

CUSHION
WITH TIES ▽

UPHOLSTERY

55 CONTRASTING FABRICS

Covering old sofas, armchairs, and dining-room chairs with new fabric will completely transform them. Choose a specific style, such as formal, modern, or ethnic, and co-ordinate the fabric colors and textures, or deliberately select contrasting colors and patterns. Skilfully done, the effect can be colorful and stunning. Scatter cushions can make visual links between different room elements.

56 MATCHING FABRICS

The easiest way to match fabrics is to choose one particular fabric and use it on two large items, such as the sofa and the curtains. Another way is to use light-colored, indistinctly patterned fabrics that combine easily with other fabrics, even if they are not exactly the same color and pattern. If you do not want the expense of re-covering upholstery, use throws to introduce new colors and textures.

MATCH SQUARES & STRIPES

CO-ORDINATE COLOR AND PATTERN

57 MEASURING FOR A SLIPCOVER

For a cover with ties measure:
- From center of one front arm to other around chair back. From floor to the center of top of an arm. Add 1 in (2.5 cm) for seams and 5 in (12.5 cm) for tie-under flap.
- From seat level to center of top of inside arms. Add 1 in (2.5 cm) for seams and 6 in (15 cm) for tuck-in.
- From seat back to front, adding 6 in (15 cm) for back tuck-in and 1 in (2.5 cm) for apron seam. Measure seat width and add 6 in (15 cm) for each side's tuck-in.
- Width of seat, plus 2 in (5 cm) by drop for apron. Allow for seams and 5 in (12.5 cm) for flap at front.

Inside arm   *Inside back*   *Outside back*

Outside arm

Seat   *Apron*   *Front arm*

58 HOW TO MAKE A CUTTING PLAN

Once you have accurate measurements, you can make a cutting plan. If you are using patterned fabric, place any motif to the center of each section. Draw the dimensions of the fabric pieces to scale on paper. Cut the fabric into rectangles; you can trim each piece to fit as you fix it around the chair. To make a slipcover (*see p.44*), follow the plan below and cut the fabric into four sections, one for the outside chair piece, one for the inside arms and back, one for the seat, and one for the apron. Pin paper labels to each piece of fabric so that you don't confuse one section with another. The arrows in the plan indicate the straight grain, along which you should always cut.

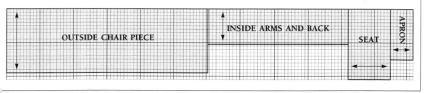

OUTSIDE CHAIR PIECE   INSIDE ARMS AND BACK   SEAT   APRON

59 HOW TO MAKE A SLIPCOVER

A slipcover is probably the simplest way to cover an old run-down chair. Although it will not fit as well as a fitted cover, it is easy to remove and clean. To help you make this one, consult the cutting plan on page 43. Make all seams 1 in (2.5 cm) in from the raw edges.

1 Mark the central point on the back edge of the seat, and the central point on the inside back piece with a vanishing-ink pen.

2 Match the central points of the pieces for the inside seat and position the two panels of fabric right sides together.

3 Sew the seat piece to the inside back piece. Trim the corners of the inside back allowance. Neaten seams with zigzag stitch.

4 Mark the central point of the front edge of the seat and the central point of the top edge of the apron. Match and sew right sides together. Snip into the seat seam allowance to turn corners at top of apron.

5 Sew the outside back piece to the inside back piece, with the right sides together. The seams should be positioned 1 in (2.5 cm) from the edges. Do not sew the front edge of the arms.

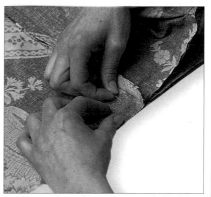

6 To sew the front edges of the arms, pin, tack, and sew the outside back piece to the inside back piece, with the right sides together. Stop when you reach the edge of the seat seam.

7 Pin, tack, and sew the outside back piece to the apron piece, with the right sides together. Make sure that the seat piece seam is turned back out of the way of the apron and back piece seam line.

8 This chair cover is not secured by ties, instead it reaches to the floor. Put the cover on the chair. Check the length and add on 1 in (2.5 cm) for a seam allowance. Mark the length with tailor's chalk and remove the cover. Turn it inside out and sew a double 1 in (2.5 cm) hem. Press.

ATTACHING THE TIES
To make this cover with ties, allow extra fabric for flaps. Fold the flaps under the chair at the sides and tie around the legs with ties.

TABLE LINEN

60 CHOOSING A TABLECLOTH

Dining-room tables, kitchen tables, and dressing and display tables can all be enhanced by the addition of a tablecloth. Achieve an elegant look by adding white linen to a table, or bring an air of cheerfulness and informality to a room with bright colors and patterns. Although there are no set rules for tablecloth lengths, dining tablecloths look best if they reach diners' knees. Display tables suit a long length of fabric.

TWO-TIER EFFECT

61 MEASURING A RECTANGULAR TABLE

When you measure for a tablecloth, take account of the drop. To determine the drop for a kitchen or dining-room table, measure from the edge of the tabletop to the seat level of a chair. For a full-length tablecloth, measure from the edge of the tabletop to the floor.

TABLE LENGTH
To calculate the length, measure the length and add twice the required drop, plus 1 in (2.5 cm) for the hem.

DROP OF CLOTH
Calculate the required drop from the edge of the table to the floor or chair level.

TABLE WIDTH
Measure the table width, add twice the required drop and add 1 in (2.5 cm) for a hem allowance.

62 HOW TO MEASURE A ROUND TABLE

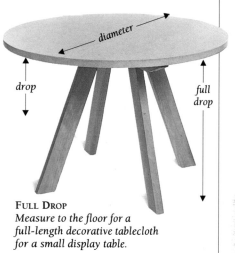

■ For a square cloth for a round table, measure the table's diameter and add twice the drop and 1 in (2.5 cm) for a hem.

■ For a rectangular cloth for an oval table, measure the table's length and add twice the drop plus 1 in (2.5 cm) for the hem. Measure in the same way for the width.

■ For an oval cloth for an oval table, make a paper template of the table top and pin it to the fabric. Add the drop requirement plus 1 in (2.5 cm) for the hem.

FULL DROP
Measure to the floor for a full-length decorative tablecloth for a small display table.

63 HOW TO CUT A CIRCULAR TABLECLOTH

Start by making a template to help you cut out the fabric correctly. First make a compass by knotting one end of a length of string around a push pin and the other end around a pencil. The compass will help you draw a perfect arc.

1 Cut out a fabric square with each side equal to the tablecloth's diameter. Fold into quarters, right sides together.

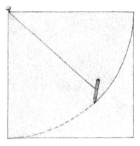

2 Cut a piece of paper to the size of the folded fabric. Draw an arc across the paper from corner to corner with the compass.

3 Cut along the line. Pin onto the fabric so that the edges align. Trace the arc onto the fabric. Cut the fabric along the arc.

64 LINEN TABLECLOTH WITH LACE EDGING

Choose a suitable lace edging. If you have an old piece of cloth with a lace edging, you can remove the lace and attach it to a new piece of linen. If you use old lace, wash it, cover it with a damp cloth, and press. Cut the fabric to fit within the lace edging, adding an extra 4 in (10 cm) all around for hems. Join the widths with flat fell seams (see p.63). You will find a triangle useful to make the corners as square as possible. Lay the linen fabric on a flat surface and place the edging around it.

LARGE TRIANGLE

SEWING SCISSORS

VANISHING-INK PEN

1 Place the triangle on the fabric and align the corners. Measure the edges to make sure that they are of equal length.

2 Mark the inner edge of the lace on the linen fabric with a vanishing-ink pen and tailor's chalk. Remove the edging.

3 To make a double hem, mark a line 4 in (10 cm) outside the first line, then another the same distance from the second.

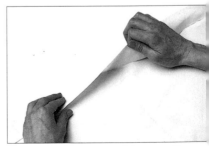

4 Cut the fabric around the outer line. Fold a 2 in (5 cm) double hem along all four edges. Press.

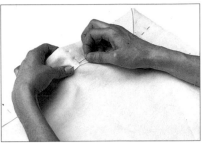

5 Unfold two layers of fabric at each corner. Fold the first turning into a miter. Press. Unfold. Trim mitered corner.

6 Refold the double hem and miter each corner. Tack ⅜ in (1 cm) from the inner edge of the hem. Slipstitch to secure.

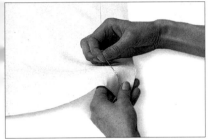

7 You can neaten the four miters at each of the corners by slipstitching the folded edges together.

8 Lay the fabric flat and tack the edging to it, using large slipstitches. Do not use pins as they could damage the lace.

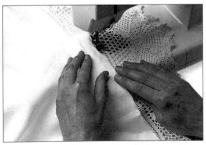

9 To secure the lace, slipstitch or machine-sew shallow zigzag stitches. Press. Remove large slipstitches.

ELEGANT LINEN TABLECLOTH

65 OILCLOTH TABLECLOTH

When making a tablecloth for regular use, such as for a kitchen table, choose a fabric that is both sturdy and easy to clean. A PVC-coated fabric or an oilcloth is easy to wipe down and is stain-resistant. Measure the table and calculate the dimension of the fabric you will need (*see pp.46–47*). Cut out the fabric and match the patterns.

1 Temporarily ladder stitch the widths together (*see p.61*). For permanent joins, use flat fell seams.

2 Fold right sides together. Sew along the seam ⅝ in (1.5 cm) from the edges. Trim one seam allowance to ¼ in (6 mm).

3 Fold the wide seam over the narrow. Tack near the seam edge. Turn right side out and machine-sew along tacking.

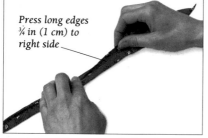

Press long edges ¾ in (1 cm) to right side

4 Make a bias strip to the length of the perimeter, by twice the edging width, plus ¾ in (2 cm) for folds (*see p.60*).

5 Open out the strip and place its right side to the right side of the tablecloth. Machine sew along the fold line.

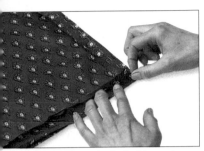

6 At the corners, pinch the bias strip and continue sewing up to, but never over, the fold. Continue sewing.

66 MAKING A NAPKIN

You can use offcuts from other fabrics to make napkins, although napkins should not be smaller than 12 in (30 cm) square. Use a strong fabric that is easy to clean.

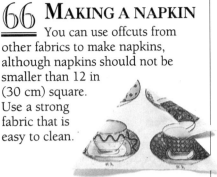

SIMPLE COTTON NAPKIN

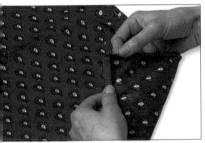

7 Miter the strips at the corners. Turn the binding over the raw edge. Sew its folded edge to the wrong side of the cloth.

1 Add 1¼ in (3 cm) to each side for double hems. Fold a double hem on all sides and press. Unfold edges.

HARD-WEARING TABLECLOTH

2 Miter the corners along the first fold. Unfold and cut across each corner. Refold and finish mitering corners. Hem.

BED LINEN

67 CONSIDER THE STYLE

Selecting bed linen is an important and personal decision since your bed forms the focal point of your bedroom. Some useful tips are:
- For a stylish, simple look, opt for plain or discreetly patterned fabric.
- Create a sumptuous look with patterned fabrics with trimmings.
- Consider the type of bed when choosing bed linen. For example, an ornate four-poster will look best with elaborate bed linen.
- Provide a dust ruffle to hide an ugly divan base.
- Add throws and cushions to unify the bed linen with the surrounding decor of the room.

MATCHING CUSHIONS & CANOPY

68 HOW TO MEASURE FOR A PILLOWCASE

This simple pillowcase is made from one continuous length of fabric. Measure the pillow length and width. Cut out the fabric to twice the length required, adding 9½ in (24 cm) for turnings and the fold-over flap (this is folded over the inside, forming a pocket). Add 1¼ in (3 cm) to the width for seam allowances.

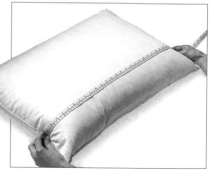

MEASURE WITH A CLOTH TAPE

69 HOW TO MAKE A PILLOWCASE

Cut the fabric, and then tack a ⅝ in (1.5 cm) double hem along the width at one end of the fabric. At the opposite end, fold over a hem to the wrong side by ⅜ in (1 cm), followed by a 2 in (5 cm) turning to form a wide-hemmed edge. Pin, tack, and sew.

1 At the other end, fold over a 6 in (15 cm) flap to the inside. Pin and press. Fold the fabric in half along the width, wrong sides together.

2 Align sides and wide-hemmed edge with flap edge. Sew a ¼ in (6 mm) seam on each long side. Trim seams. Turn wrong side out and press.

3 Tack long sides of fabric together ⅜ in (1 cm) from the first seam. Machine sew long sides ⅜ in (1 cm) from the first seam. Turn right side out.

70 MEASURING FOR A DUST RUFFLE

Measure the length and width of bed and take off 8 in (20 cm) all around. Cut out fabric for the top panel to this size. Cut out fabric for the skirt to three times the length of the top panel, plus one-and-a-half times its width, by the skirt drop. Cut out five strips, all 5 in (12.5 cm) wide. Two strips should be the length of A, plus 1¼ in (3 cm); two should be the length of B, minus 9¼ in (23 cm); and one should be the length of B, plus 1¼ in (3 cm) for the facing.

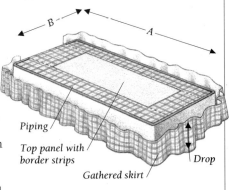

Piping

Top panel with border strips

Gathered skirt

Drop

DIMENSIONS FOR GATHERED RUFFLE

71 HOW TO MAKE A DUST RUFFLE

Measure and cut out the fabric pieces following the instructions on page 53. To economize, use a plain fabric for the unseen top panel.

1 ▷ Sew a short strip to all sides of the top panel, right sides together, ¾ in (1.5 cm) from the edges. Press seams open.

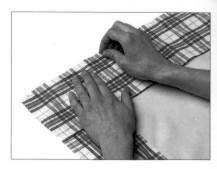

2 △ Attach a long border strip to each side of the top panel. Draw around a glass. Cut along the curve at each corner.

3 Define the edge between the border and the skirt with either contrasting or matching piping if desired. Instructions for making piping are given on page 60. If you add piping, it should be tacked to the right side of the top panel, with the extra turned around the head end corners.

4 Turn a ⅜ in (1.5 cm) double hem at the ends and bottom edge of the skirt. Press. Pin, tack, and sew the hems. On the top edge of the fabric, measuring from one hemmed end, mark a point at one-and-a-half times the length of A (see p.53).

5 From this point, measure one-and-a-half times the length of B and mark. The remaining length fits the other side.

6 Sew gathering stitches between the marks along the top of the skirt, ⅜ in (1.5 cm) from the edge.

7 Align one end of the skirt with one end of top seam, right sides together. Pin ⅝ in (1.5 cm) from the edge.

8 Match the first mark to the first corner. Pin. Pull up the gathers. Repeat along all sections of the skirt. Sew in place.

9 On one long edge of the facing strip turn and sew a double hem of ³⁄₁₆ in (5 mm) followed by ⅜ in (1 cm).

10 Sew the raw edge of the facing to the head end of the top panel, right sides together, along the skirt seams.

◁ **FINISHING & FITTING**
Turn right side out. The facing strip lies over the head end of the top panel, neatening the appearance. Press the dust ruffle and then fit over the bed. To save on expense, this ruffle has a plain top panel.

GATHERED RUFFLE ▷

72 SHEET WITH DECORATIVE STITCHING

Flat sheets are more versatile than fitted sheets since they can be used as both top and bottom sheets. Measure the length and width of the mattress. Add 16 in (40 cm) to the width, plus twice the mattress depth. Add 20 in (50 cm) to the length, and ¾ in (2 cm) for the side hems.

1 Sew double hems to the wrong side along long edges and ⅝ in (1.5 cm) along the base edge.

2 At the top edge of the sheet, turn and tack a 2 in (5 cm) double hem to the wrong side.

3 Machine stitch the wide hem edge with a close zigzag stitch. Undo the tacking stitches. Press.

73 SHEET WITH PIPING

Make the sheet as above. Topstitch ⅜ in (1 cm) from the edge of the wide hem. Topstitch again ½ in (12 mm) from the first row. Thread the piping through the channel. Oversew ends to secure.

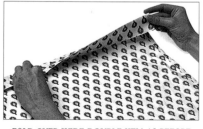

FOLD OVER WIDE DOUBLE HEM AS BEFORE

74 MEASURING FOR A DUVET COVER

You can make a simple cover from just one length of fabric. When measuring, bear in mind that your duvet should overlap either side of your bed by about 10 in (25 cm). Measure the length and width of your duvet. Cut out a piece of fabric twice the length of the duvet plus 6 in (15 cm) and the width of the duvet plus 4 in (10 cm). These allowances are for seams and fastenings and also provide space for the duvet, which is particularly important if it is filled with feathers and down.

75 DUVET COVER

Turn under short sides by ⅜ in (1 cm) and then ⅝ in (1.5 cm) to the wrong side. Sew hems. Fold in half, wrong sides together. Align hemmed edges. Sew down each side ³⁄₁₆ in (5 mm) from the edges. Trim allowance to ⅛ in (3 mm) along sides. Turn wrong sides out and press. Finish seam at each side ⅜ in (1 cm) from the folded edge.

Mark opening 2 in (5 cm) from folded edge of the opening

1 Mark opening on wrong sides of fabric along both sides of the cover.

2 From the edge of each cover, sew 8 in (20 cm) along the mark. Fold both unsewn edges at the opening end to the wrong side along the marked guidelines.

3 Press the folded edges. Turn the cover right side out and press again. Mark positions of buttonholes along one edge of opening.

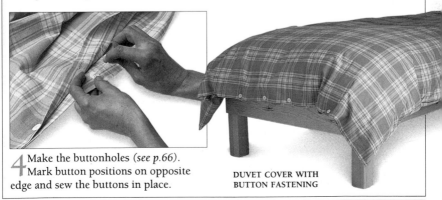

4 Make the buttonholes (see p.66). Mark button positions on opposite edge and sew the buttons in place.

DUVET COVER WITH BUTTON FASTENING

SEWING & FABRIC TIPS

76 SEWING KIT

For a professional finish, you will need proper equipment. Once you have assembled your kit, use it for sewing only.

SEWING THREADS

NEEDLES

PENCIL

TACKING THREAD

THREADER

PINS

PIN CUSHION

VANISHING-INK PEN

LARGE TRIANGLE

CLOTH TAPE MEASURE

TAILOR'S CHALK

STRAIGHT STITCH FOOT

ZIPPER FOOT

TWIN & SINGLE NEEDLES

MACHINE BOBBINS

△ **MEASURING & MARKING**
Use accurate measuring equipment and markers that can be easily rubbed off. Align corners with triangles.

PINKING SHEARS

UPHOLSTERY NEEDLE

UPHOLSTERY SKEWER

EMBROIDERY SCISSORS

SEWING MACHINE

SEWING SCISSORS

SEAM RIPPER

CLOTHES PEGS

BODKIN

△ **SCISSORS & OTHER USEFUL TOOLS**
Cut fabric with sharp scissors. Use embroidery scissors for intricate cutting.

△ **SEWING & MACHINE ACCESSORIES**
It is faster and easier to use a sewing machine than to sew by hand. Modern machines have a range of accessories.

77 FABRIC CHOICE

Apart from natural fibers, such as wool, silk, and cotton, a wide range of blended and synthetic fabrics is available. These are easier to care for and stronger than natural fibers.

◁ **LINING FABRIC**
Use cotton sateen for lining curtains, and calico for lining inner covers.

SHEER FABRICS
Lightweight fabrics, such as muslin, voile, and lace can be used for translucent window dressings or for decorative edgings. They can be difficult to work with.

LIGHTWEIGHT FABRICS
These include fine cottons and silks. They can be translucent, so if you want to use one as a curtain fabric, line it to protect it from harsh sunlight.

LIGHT- TO MEDIUM-WEIGHT FABRICS
These have a finely woven texture and yet are strong and hardwearing. Use them for window dressings, bed furnishings, cushion covers, and table linen.

MEDIUM-WEIGHT FABRICS
These constitute the majority of furnishing fabrics and include linen, wool, and cotton mixes, and mixes of natural and synthetic fibers. Many are suitable for upholstery.

HEAVYWEIGHT FABRICS
These are hardwearing and are often used for upholstery. They include chenille, velvet, and wool and cotton mixes. They can be difficult to work with and to shape.

78 MAKING PIPING FROM BIAS STRIPS

First make a bias strip by folding the fabric diagonally so that one straight edge lies parallel to the adjacent edge. Press. Measure the lines parallel to the bias crease and cut the strips. To join strips, place at right angles to each other and sew ¼ in (5 mm) from the raw edge. Buy the piping cord and wash to pre-shrink. Cut a bias strip to the circumference of the cord, adding 1¼ in (3 cm) for seams. Lay the cord along the center of the wrong side of the strip. Fold the strip and sew near the cord. If you use a machine, work with a zipper attachment.

79 NEATENING RAW EDGES

Raw edges of fabric must be finished to prevent them from fraying. This is particularly important for furnishings that have to endure hard wear. There are several ways of neatening raw edges. The easiest are pinking or zigzag machine stitch. Overlocking, oversewing, and bias binding are alternatives.

◁ **PINKING SHEARS**
Use pinking shears to cut a serrated edge. Although an easy technique, a pinked edge can fray easily.

MACHINE ZIGZAG
Use the zigzag stitch accessory on your sewing machine. Stitch as near to the edge as possible.

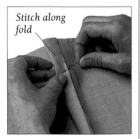

Stitch along fold

OVERSEWING BY HAND
Make evenly spaced stitches from the back to the front of the fabric. Do not pull the stitches too tight.

BIAS BINDING
Align unfolded edge of binding to raw edge. Sew along fold. Fold over edge and sew through all layers.

OVERLOCKING
Allow 1 in (2.5 cm) for seams. Sew. Trim one seam to ¼ in (5 mm). Fold wide edge, tuck raw edge under.

80 HOW TO SLIPSTITCH

This stitch is usually used for hems or where a seam must be sewn from the right side of the fabric, for example, where you close a cushion cover opening. Start by taking the needle across the opening. Make the first stitch 1/16 in (2 mm) long in the seam-line fold. Bring the thread back across the opening and make a similar stitch in the first side. Do this to the end. Fasten off in the seam.

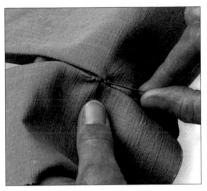

SLIPSTITCH TO CLOSE A GAP

81 HOW TO LADDER STITCH

Ladder stitching is a method of joining panels of patterned fabric and ensuring that the fabric pattern matches exactly across the seam before it is permanently sewn. The fabric pieces are tacked together from the patterned, right side. When you match the pattern over the panels you may waste some fabric, but the professional finish achieved is worthwhile. You will need an iron for this technique. Start by laying the fabric panels right side up, and overlapping the edges.

1 Fold the edge of the top piece under by 3/4 in (2 cm) or more for a heavy fabric. Press the fold. Align the pattern and pin.

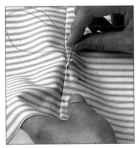

2 Secure the end of the thread on the seam line. Make a stitch 3/8 in (1 cm) long inside the seam fold in the top piece.

3 Make another stitch in the bottom piece. Sew to the seam end. Fold right sides together. Sew. Remove ladder stitches.

82 FLAT SEAMS

This is the most useful method of joining fabric. Always pin and tack before sewing. Secure the thread by sewing backward and forward along the seam line for ⅜ in (1 cm) several times. Finish in the same way.

SIMPLE PLAIN FLAT SEAMS

83 HOW TO NOTCH FABRIC

If you need to join fabric pieces from the bottom edge to the top edge, you can identify the direction of the lengths by cutting notches at the top edge. This will also ensure that the pile runs in the same direction.

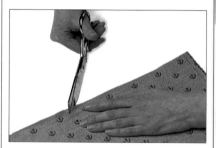

CUT NOTCHES AT TOP EDGE

84 HOW TO CLIP NOTCHES

Create neat corners and curves by cutting and clipping. At a corner, cut away a triangle of fabric. An outward curve should be clipped, an inward curve notched.

△ CLIPPING CORNERS
Cut across the seam allowance. Leave about ¼ in (6 mm) between the seam and the cut edge of the fabric.

◁ CLIPPING CURVES
Clip a convex curve into the serrated edge seen here. If concave, snip into the seam allowance, but not too close to the seam.

85 HOW TO HEM BY HERRINGBONE

With the folded edge of the fabric facing toward you, hold the needle above the hem, pointing from left to right. Pick up threads from the flat fabric. Bring the needle under the fold and up. Repeat to the left.

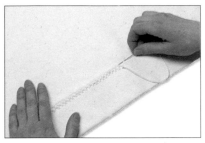

CROSS EACH STITCH OVER THE LAST

86 PLACING JOINS

Before joining fabric panels, consider where the joins should be positioned in relation to the finished product. Useful guidelines to follow are: on curtains, place the joins to the sides; on bed and table linen, place a complete panel down the middle length.

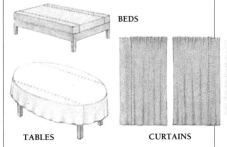

BEDS

TABLES   CURTAINS

87 FLAT FELL SEAMS

Use flat fell seams to achieve a strong, flat finish, which is very useful on upholstery. These seams conceal the raw edges of the fabric, although their stitching is visible on the right side of the fabric.

1 Sew right sides together, ⅝ in (1.5 cm) from the edge. Trim one edge to 3/16 in (5 mm).

2 Fold the wide seam over the narrow. Lay both to one side, enclose the raw edge, and tack.

3 Sew along the tacking line from the right side and press the seam flat. A row of stitches will show.

88 MEASURING & MARKING

There are occasions when you need to mark fabric, for example, when you want to cut it out. Some useful guidelines are as follows:

■ Always lay the fabric out flat on a smooth and steady surface.

■ Use a vanishing-ink pen or tailor's chalk to mark fabric, as neither leave permanent marks. Tailor's chalk is sold in a variety of colors and is available in pencil form and in flat pieces.

■ There are various types of measure. Fiberglass and linen tape measures are the most accurate as they barely stretch.

89 PATTERNED FABRICS

Measure the pattern repeat and match the pattern across seams. Cut the first width. Cut the second after matching to the first. Secure panels and machine stitch with ladder stitch.

TRY TO MATCH PATTERNS ACROSS SEAMS

90 JOINING PLAIN FABRICS

To make soft furnishings, you will nearly always need to join fabric panels together. You can join panels with plain flat seams (see p.62). For a strong, flat finish use flat fell seams (see p.63).

1 Lay panels right sides together. Match raw edges. Pin and tack, making a ⅝ in (1.5 cm) seam from the edges.

2 Remove pins. Machine-sew along the tacking. (Use either plain flat seams or flat fell seams.) Remove tacking stitches.

3 Open the seam allowance and press it flat. For a professional finish, sew down the entire length of the seam.

91 HOW TO MITER CORNERS

Mitering hems at corners ensures that the final hem will be neat. It should be done before the hem is sewn. If the fabric in the corners is bulky, cut some of the excess fabric from the miters.

1 Neaten the raw edges. Fold the hems, one over the other, and press. Mark the points where they cross with pins.

2 Unfold the hem. Make a fold across the corner from one pin to the other (the creases should align). Press the fold.

3 Refold the hems over the diagonally folded corner. Slipstitch the corner folds together. Sew the hem as required.

92 WHICH FASTENING?

Below are examples of the simplest fastenings to attach to home furnishings. Snaps and Velcro are easily hidden within a seam. Some hooks and eyes are strong enough to take considerable strain.

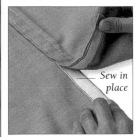

Sew in place

Sew through loop

VELCRO
Easy-to-use Velcro is too stiff for lightweight fabric. Use a tape slightly narrower than the seam allowance.

SEW-ON SNAPS
These are available in metal and plastic. Some are sold loose, others mounted onto a tape.

HOOKS & EYES
These can be as strong as a zipper. They are suitable for edge-to-edge or over-lapping fabric pieces.

93 HOW TO MAKE TIES

Flat fabric ties make good decorative fastenings for lightweight furnishings, especially for cushions and bed furnishings. Cut the length you desire and twice the width, plus ⅜ in (1 cm) all around.

1 △ Fold the edges of the long sides together to the wrong side by ⅜ in (1 cm). Press. Cut the corners diagonally. Fold the ends to the wrong side.

2 Press. Fold in half lengthways, right side out. Sew all sides ⅟₁₆ in (2 mm) from the edge. Make up the other tie. Pin in place before sewing.

94 HOW TO HAND SEW A BUTTONHOLE

Sew in fine blanket stitch with buttonhole thread. Insert the needle below the edge, with the point straight up and then loop the thread behind the point. Draw the thread to lie along the top of the edge.

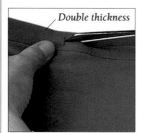

Double thickness

1 Mark the position. Use a seam ripper to cut open the buttonhole. Make the fastening edge from a double thickness of fabric.

2 Secure the thread at one end of the slit. Start at the end that will take the strain. Oversew across this end.

3 Sew closely along one side in fine blanket stitch ⅛ in (3 mm) from the end. Oversew at the far end. Sew the other side.

95 HOW TO ADD A FRINGE IN A SEAM

Check that the fringe is colorfast and preshrunk. If there are "stay" stitches on the fringe edge, leave them in. Lay the fringe facedown on the right side of the fabric. Align the part you will sew through with the seam. Tack in place. Lay the second panel of fabric right-side down on the first. Tack through all layers. Sew and turn right side out.

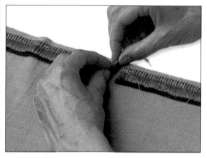

BUTT THE ENDS OF ANY JOINS

96 MAKING BOWS

Cut a strip of fabric to the length and to double the finished width required, adding ¾ in (2 cm) all around for the seam. Fold in half lengthways. Sew ⅜ in (1 cm) from the raw edge. Leave a gap in the center for turning right side out. Sew across the ends diagonally. Snip the seam allowances at the corners. Turn right side out and press. Slipstitch the opening closed and tie in a bow.

SNIP THE SEAM ALLOWANCES

97 ALTERNATIVE WAYS TO HEM

Sometimes you may not have the time to stitch an item properly. Here are a few alternative measures. Fusible bonding is a web-like strip of adhesive. Place it between the two fabric layers of a hem. Press the hem and the strip will adhere to the fabric, keeping the hem in place. Tacking tape, a narrow, two-sided sticky tape, is a more temporary measure. It can be useful for testing out the length of curtain hems before stitching them. It can also be used as an alternative to tacking where two wrong sides need to be held together. Check the manufacturer's instructions before using either method.

FUSIBLE BONDING

TACKING TAPE

CARE & CLEANING

98 HOW TO CARE FOR SOFT FURNISHINGS

When you buy fabric, it will probably have its cleaning requirements displayed on a label or along the selvage. Make a note of the manufacturer's advice. If there are no cleaning instructions, the safest course of action is dry cleaning. Cleaning and protection from heat or sunlight will preserve the color and condition of your fabric creations.

TAKE CARE OF YOUR FABRIC

99 HOW TO CLEAN CURTAINS

Remove the curtains from the hanging system. Flatten out the heading tape and shake to remove the surface dust. If washable, soak curtains in cold water for about ten minutes with a small quantity of detergent. Rinse and wash the curtains as recommended. Rehang sheer and net curtains when they are still slightly damp.

△ **REMOVE THE CURTAIN HOOKS**
Once you have taken the curtains down, remove all the hooks from the heading tape.

△ **UNTIE THE KNOT**
Untie the knot at the end of the tape and gently pull the heading tape flat.

100 HOW TO CLEAN LOOSE COVERS

Clean the cover with a vacuum cleaner while it is in place. This removes surface dust. If there are pet hairs, dab the area with sticky tape. Remove the cover and wash by hand, by machine, or dry clean (check the fabric manufacturer's instructions). When dry, refit the cover, and if necessary press it when in place through a clean layer of fabric.

◁ **CLEAN CUSHION COVERS**
Secure any fastenings on the cover before washing. Hang to dry and press when the fabric is slightly damp.

REFIT COVER & PRESS

101 HOW TO REMOVE STAINS

Below are a number of useful remedies that successfully treat most common stains.

■ For greasy or oil stains, scrape off the residue with a knife and blot the fabric with tissue. Treat with a grease solvent.

■ For blood, sponge with cold, salted water. Soak and wash with a detergent. Rinse well.

■ For coffee and tea, mop up remaining liquid immediately. Soak the affected area in a warm solution of detergent. If necessary, when the fabric is dry, clean with a stain remover.

■ For wine, do not let the stain dry. Mop up the wine and soak the area in tepid water. Alternatively, apply talcum powder, leaving it to absorb the wine for 12 hours. Vacuum the powder and, finally, wash with a detergent.

■ For paint and varnish, dab off any excess and sponge with cold water. Wash as recommended. If varnish or oil-based paint, scrape away residue and apply turpentine or a paint remover.

■ For candle wax, remove the excess wax. Sandwich between two layers of brown paper or blotting paper and pass a warm iron over. Remove any remaining stains with a grease solvent.

■ For chewing gum, hold a bag of ice cubes over the area. When the gum is hard, pick off from the fabric.

INDEX

ACKNOWLEDGMENTS

Dorling Kindersley would like to thank Julia Pashley for picture research, Hilary Bird for compiling the index, Ann Kay for proof-reading, Gloria Horsfall for design assistance, Cooling Brown for editorial assistance, and Mark Bracey for computer assistance.

Photography
KEY: t *top*; b *bottom*; c *center*; l *left*; r *right*
All photographs by Tim Ridley except for:

Robert Harding Syndication/IPC Magazines
Bill Batten 52tr; Dominic Blackmore 6tr, 9cl, 42bl

Elizabeth Whiting Associates
2, 8cr, 9tr, 42br

Illustrations
Andrew MacDonald